D1403723

What Does a CITIZEN Do?

What Does a Juror Do?

Enslow Publishing
101 W. 23rd Street
Suite 240
New York, NY 10011
USA
enslow.com

Bridey Heing

Published in 2019 by Enslow Publishing, LLC.
101 W. 23rd Street, Suite 240, New York, NY 10011

Library of Congress Cataloging-in-Publication Data

Names: Heing, Bridey, author.
Title: What does a juror do? / Bridey Heing.
Description: New York : Enslow Publishing, LLC. , [2019] | Series: What does a citizen do? | Includes bibliographical references and index. | Audience: Grades 5–8.
Identifiers: LCCN 2017055220| ISBN 9780766098633 (library bound) | ISBN 9780766098640 (pbk.)
Subjects: LCSH: Jury—United States—Juvenile literature. | Jurors—United States—Juvenile literature. | Fair trial—United States—Juvenile literature.
Classification: LCC KF8972 .H45 2018 | DDC 347.73/752—dc23
LC record available at https://lccn.loc.gov/2017055220

Printed in the United States of America

To Our Readers: We have done our best to make sure all website addresses in this book were active and appropriate when we went to press. However, the author and the publisher have no control over and assume no liability for the material available on those websites or on any websites they may link to. Any comments or suggestions can be sent by e-mail to customerservice@enslow.com.

Photo Credits: Cover, p. 1 Fuse/Corbis/Getty Images; p. 4 P_Wei/E+/Getty Images; pp. 6–7 Alan Klehr/The Image Bank/Getty Images; p. 8 Anastasios71/Shutterstock. com; p. 10 eddtoro/Shutterstock.com; p. 12 Gundam_Ai/Shutterstock.com; p. 15 Fotosearch/Archive Photos/Getty Images; p. 18 James Steidl/Shutterstock.com; p. 20 Dennis MacDonald/Alamy Stock Photo; p. 22 United Archives GmbH/Alamy Stock Photo; p. 25 Guy Cali/Corbis/Getty Images; p. 27 Hero Images/Getty Images; pp. 32–33 © iStockphoto.com/RichLegg; pp. 34–35 Image Source Plus/Alamy Stock Photo; pp. 36, 40 sirtravelalot/Shutterstock.com; p. 42 Ted Soqui/Sygma/Getty Images; p. 44 Joshua Lott/Getty Images.

CONTENTS

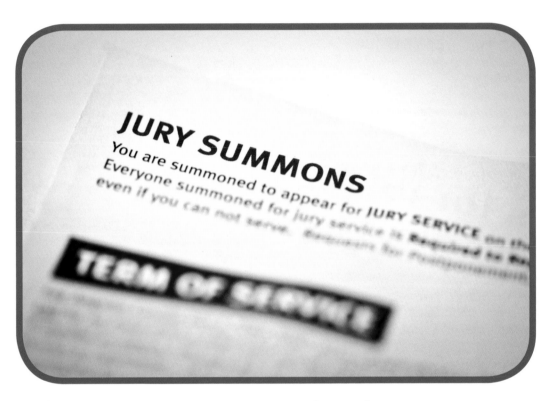

JURY SUMMONS
You are summoned to appear for JURY SERVICE on the
Everyone summoned for jury service is **Required to** Re
even if you can not serve. Re

After you receive a jury summons in the mail, you must report to a designated courthouse to be considered for jury service.

Introduction

The average citizen interacts with the government in many ways, but one of the most important is serving on a jury. A jury, which is a panel of men and women who hear a case and decide together whether someone accused of a crime is guilty or not guilty, is an important part of the justice system. They help ensure a fair and balanced trial, and being able to be tried by a jury is one of the most fundamental rights guaranteed to us by the US Constitution.

The right to a jury trial is first mentioned in the Constitution in Article III: "The Trial of all Crimes, except in Cases of Impeachment, shall be by Jury." It is further explained in the Bill of Rights. The Sixth Amendment reads in part, "In all criminal prosecutions, the accused shall enjoy the right to a speedy and public trial, by an impartial jury of the state and district wherein the crime shall have been committed." This means that all people convicted of crimes for which they could be punished with over six months in prison have the opportunity to have their case heard by a jury. For cases in which the likely punishment is fewer than six months in

While the number can vary, juries typically require six to twelve jurors, who hear evidence on civil or criminal matters and then decide on a verdict.

prison, states can decide if a jury trial can take place. But not all trials have to be heard by juries; the accused can also choose to have his or her case heard only by a judge, who then reaches a verdict based on evidence presented by the defense and the prosecution.

Jurors, or the people who make up the jury, are selected from lists put together by states. Most often these lists include current voter registration or driver's license rolls. For federal courts, jurors are selected from voter registrations. In all cases, the selection process is random, an important part of making sure juries are fair and unbiased, and many states have limits on how often someone can be called for jury duty. For example, in the District of Columbia a registered voter can be called only once in a two-year period, although it is possible that he or she will not be called at all in that timeframe.

Jurors are tasked with hearing all the evidence and arguments of a case, deliberating in private, and coming to a verdict. But while that may sound simple, it's actually a complicated process with strict guidelines and rules to ensure juries hand down verdicts that are fair and have legal standing. Jurors are a key part of a system that is constantly evolving and adapting to meet the needs of the people. In this book, we'll learn more about what jurors do within the justice system. We'll also learn about how juries have evolved over time, as well as important reforms taking place to ensure that all trials are fair and all juries are unbiased.

One of the most famous jury trials in ancient Greece involved the philosopher Socrates, who was sentenced to death.

The History of the Jury

Today, juries are one of the defining features of our justice system. We're used to seeing jurors on TV and in movies, and most of us are familiar with what parts of the process look like. But even though juries are common today, the way they fit into the justice system has evolved over time. Juries, and who is allowed to serve on them, have changed a lot over the course of recent history, and those changes reflect the expansion of civil rights that has taken place in that time.

The Ancient Roots of Juries

The concept of a jury is nothing new. In ancient Greece, juries heard arguments in Athens much as they do today, but, according to the ancient philosopher Aristotle, they based their verdicts on their own understandings of justice. These juries were made up of at least five hundred citizens, and they decided their verdicts based on the majority of those on the jury rather than the unanimous decision we require today. A similar system developed under the Roman Empire, with standing juries established to hear specific kinds of cases.

Depending on the kind of jury summons they receive, jurors report to a municipal (city or county), state, or federal courthouse to be considered for jury service.

Juries were introduced in England in the twelfth century by King Henry II. He put in place a court system that had panels of twelve men who heard cases regarding land disputes. He also introduced grand juries, or panels of jurors that identified potential crimes and criminals, who were then put to trial by ordeal. When trial by ordeal fell out of favor in 1215, grand juries were used to determine verdicts as well. The year 1215 also saw a significant step in juries becoming part of citizens' rights when mention of trial by jury was included in the Magna Carta, which reads in part:

> No free man shall be captured or imprisoned or disseised of his free-hold or of his liberties, or of his free customs, or be outlawed or exiled or in any way destroyed, nor will we proceed against him by force or proceed against him by arms, but by the lawful judgment of his peers or by the law of the land.

Since then, juries have been a consistent part of justice systems around the world, changing over time into the system we know today.

Toward a Modern System

The earliest system of laws in the United States was established based on English common law, which included the right to trial by jury. Distant from English authority, colonies set up their own justice systems that relied on juries to help decide cases. When the thirteen colonies decided to revolt against England, they even based part of their argument for independence on access to trial by jury, writing in the Declaration of Independence that King George III was "depriving us in many cases, of the benefits of trial by jury."

When it came time to form their own government, the Founders decided to make the right to a trial by jury a cornerstone of the justice system. Thomas Jefferson said in 1789, "I consider trial by jury as the only anchor ever yet imagined by man, by which a government can be held to the principles of its constitution."[1] For the Founders, trial by jury was a way to ensure the government was kept in check and to ensure all citizens were treated equally in the eyes of the law.

The right to trial by jury is enshrined multiple times in the Constitution and Bill of Rights. In Article III of the Constitution, which

Since hearing evidence requires concentration and attention, jurors are either prohibited from bringing their cell phones into the courtroom or required to keep them on silent mode.

sets out the judiciary system, trial by jury is made the norm for all trials held at the federal level, with the exception of impeachment cases. It reads in part: "The Trial of all Crimes, except in Cases of Impeachment; shall be by Jury; and such Trial shall be held in the State where the said Crimes shall have been committed; but when not committed within any State, the Trial shall be at such Place or Places as the Congress may by Law have directed."

The Bill of Rights features the right to a trial by jury twice. The first instance is in the Sixth Amendment, which explains the rights of those convicted of crimes. It specifically calls for a "speedy and public trial, by an impartial jury." The Seventh Amendment preserves the right to a jury in civil cases, or those that are between private individuals or organizations rather than the state. It also states that a decision made by a jury cannot be called into question, unless special criteria are met. It reads, "In Suits at common law, where

A Citizen's Responsibility

Serving on a jury is an opportunity to take part in the justice system, but it is also an important responsibility. When someone receives a jury summons, which states when and where they are to report for jury duty, it means they have been selected randomly from the list of potential jurors. Missing jury duty is a crime, and there are consequences for simply not showing up. Some people find it difficult or economically challenging to serve on a jury, but even in those cases they must communicate with or show up to the courthouse. Consequences for missing jury duty vary by state but include fines or jail time. It's a reminder that serving as a juror is more than just a privilege; it's a duty.

the value in controversy shall exceed twenty dollars, the right of trial by jury shall be preserved, and no fact tried by a jury, shall be otherwise re-examined in any Court of the United States, than according to the rules of the common law."

Ensuring Justice

Juries have been an important part of the justice system since the earliest days of our country, but that doesn't mean that these panels have not changed with time. Juries intersect with a number of the most charged and important concepts in a democracy: citizenship, justice, equality, and impartiality. The changes that juries have undergone have been driven by some of the most crucial debates in US history, including women's rights and civil rights.

The Fourteenth Amendment, which was ratified in 1868, is an example of how juries were shaped by a changing country. Following the Civil War, citizenship was expanded to include former slaves. It extended the full protection of the law to all citizens under the Equal Protection Clause, but when it was passed this was not interpreted to extend to women or people of color. The eventually overturned Civil Rights Act of 1875 addressed this, reading in part, "That no citizen possessing all other qualification which are or may be prescribed by law shall be disqualified for service as grand or petit juror in any court of the United States, or of any State, on account of race, color, or previous condition of servitude." It wasn't until the Supreme Court case *Strauder v. West Virginia* in 1880 that it was decided the exclusion of people of color from jury service was a violation of the Equal Protection Clause for people of color accused of crimes. But it would take decades for

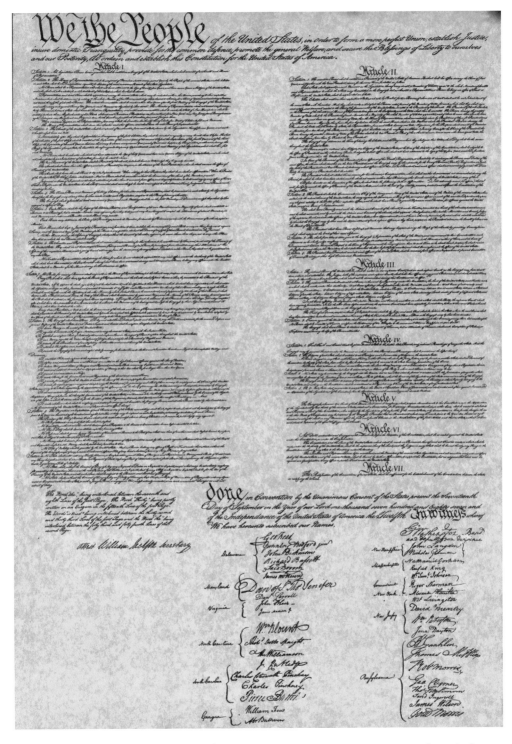

The Sixth Amendment to the Constitution guarantees the right to trial by jury in the United States.

people of color to have full access to both impartial juries and the right to serve on a jury.

The experiences of people of color as they tried to secure the right to trial by jury and the right to serve on a jury highlights the important place juries have in the justice system and the long road to ensuring that juries are able to fulfill that role. As we'll learn in chapters to come, controversy about who is able to serve on a jury and how those duties are carried out has continued into the modern day.

A Day as a Juror

The history of juries is long and complicated, but what does it mean to actually be a juror? When someone is called for jury duty, they receive a summons in the mail well in advance of the date on which they need to report to the court. This card will have the time and place where the juror needs to report, as well as any other information needed for that day. Some states require online registration before the specified date for jury duty, while others include an identification card that is needed to sign in that day.

While the sign-in process is fairly uniform across courts, the course a juror's day might take can vary widely. It all depends on the needs of the court, the regulations in place, and a bit of chance.

Arriving at the Court

When a juror gets to the court, they will be told to go to a special room where they can check in. Depending on the size of the court and the jury pool, the juror might need to wait in line with others who are also checking in. This is because courts call more jurors than they need for the day; in some places, they call a handful

Though entering the courthouse might seem intimidating, checking in for jury service is a simple process.

more, while in other places they call a set number to have available throughout the day.

Checking in is simple. Jurors provide identification and their summons, then answer a few questions before being assigned a juror number and being directed to a juror lounge. The lounge may have reading material or televisions, and there is often a period when the details of jury duty are outlined. This can be a handout or a video. If jurors have been called for a specific trial, rather than to be available for panels throughout the day, they will be briefed on the case by a judge.

This is as far as many jurors get. Because many courts call in more people than they need, a lot of jurors are dismissed before being selected for jury duty. Being called in fulfills the requirement for serving on jury duty, meaning that even if a juror isn't selected, they will not be called for jury duty again for a set period of time.

Voir Dire

Jury selection depends on court practices. In some courts, a group is selected randomly from the pool of jurors who have signed in; in other courts, everyone who comes in is briefed on the case and jurors are selected from that pool. For those who are selected for jury duty, the next step of the process is called voir dire. This is probably familiar, even if the name isn't. It's the process during which both attorneys ask questions to determine if a juror is biased one way or the other, knows either party involved in the suit, or is otherwise not able to be fair and impartial. Either attorney is able to dismiss a potential juror during this process. For those who aren't selected during voir dire, it's back to the juror's lounge for further directions or dismissal.

After lawyers complete the questioning process, or voir dire, jurors are sworn in and begin to hear evidence.

A Day in Court

Those who are selected to serve on the jury are sworn in, or empaneled, and given basic instructions from the judge. This includes listening to all evidence before making a decision on the case and not talking to anyone about the case. The jury then hears the case, with possible time outside of the court while the attorneys present arguments or motions to the judge. When that takes place, jurors wait in a private jurors' lounge, where they are not to discuss

Kemner v. Monsanto : The Longest Jury Trial in US History

The average jury trial lasts for a few days, with some lasting only one. But in 1984, a trial began that would last over three years, ending in 1987. The case, known as *Kemner v. Monsanto*, is the longest jury trial in US history. It was brought by Frances Kemner and a group of sixty-four other plaintiffs who claimed they were poisoned after a train derailment in 1979. The train was carrying a wood preservative made by Monsanto, a major American agriculture and biotechnology company, with just a small amount of dioxin, which is extremely poisonous. Described as less than a teaspoon, the amount present in the preservative that spilled near Sturgeon, Missouri, didn't make the case any less complex. Over 180 witnesses were called, and the jury deliberated for more than two months before finding that while Monsanto did not cause them any harm by exposing them to dioxin, the company was guilty of not ensuring that dioxin was eliminated as a byproduct in its plants. After the plaintiffs were awarded $1 each and $16.2 million in punitive damages, Monsanto went on to appeal the decision and it was overturned.[1]

the case even with each other. If the trial goes longer than one day, the jurors might be made to stay in a hotel to ensure they do not discuss the trial with anyone, including family.

The bulk of a juror's day, however, consists of listening to the evidence of the case at hand. This can mean listening to witnesses be cross-examined by attorneys, looking at images or objects that are presented in court, or listening to the attorneys' statements. This continues until both attorneys give their closing statements and the judge asks the jury to deliberate in private.

Jury deliberation can sometimes lead to long discussions, like in *12 Angry Men*, an acclaimed movie about a deadlocked jury.

Deliberation

Deliberation is one of the most important parts of a juror's time in court. After all the evidence in a case is presented, the jurors are sent to a private room to discuss the case and come to a verdict. To do so, they talk about the evidence, consider the laws in question, and declare whether they feel the defendant is guilty or not guilty. In order for a verdict to be reached, all jurors must agree. This unanimous decision is sometimes difficult to reach and requires extensive debate between jurors. In some cases, deliberation can last multiple days before all jurors agree. But sometimes even hours of discussion doesn't result in agreement. That results in a hung jury, and a mistrial is declared. The case is then heard again with a new jury.

Although the jury is responsible for deciding a verdict, it does not handle sentencing. This is left to the judge, who considers all the facts of the case, the jury's verdict, and other information that informs the decision. A jury is not supposed to consider punishment at all when it reaches its verdict; it is only supposed to consider the case itself, not the possible consequences of its verdict.

Being a juror comes with a lot of responsibility. All of what we've just learned can happen in one day, over the course of a week, or even over multiple months. It all depends on the case being heard. But once a jury has delivered its verdict to the court, everyone is free to go home knowing they have done their duty as citizens.

Reaching a Verdict

As we learned in the last chapter, deliberation and reaching a verdict is one of the most important parts of a juror's role in court. While listening to the evidence and paying careful attention is crucial, reaching a verdict is what the jury is meant to do at the end of the case. There are careful guidelines to ensure not only that a decision is reached, but that the decision is as fair as possible.

Of course, not all decisions reached by juries are accurate, and through the appeals process they can be overturned. In some cases, evidence eventually proves that someone convicted by a jury is innocent, proving that even in cases where a verdict is reached, it all depends on the evidence presented. So what does a jury look for when deciding a case?

Avoiding Outside Influence

As we learned, jurors are asked a series of questions before being sworn in to assure they do not have pre-existing ideas or opinions about anyone involved in the case or the possible guilt of the

Once deliberation is complete, the jurors are called back into the courtroom and the jury foreperson reads the verdict aloud.

defendant. This is an important first step in ensuring the trial is conducted fairly and the verdict reached is shaped only by evidence heard in court. But there are more restrictions put on jurors to make sure outside influence isn't introduced during the trial that could sway them in reaching a verdict.

Jurors are barred from discussing the case with each other or with anyone outside of the court, including family and friends.

This is to keep them from considering a possible verdict before all evidence is heard. Jurors are also barred from visiting the crime scene or speaking to anyone involved with either party in the trial. Although some judges do not allow note taking, most states permit jurors to take notes to use during deliberation. Jurors are not allowed to conduct independent research regarding the case or evidence—even using the internet to look up information about it is restricted.

All of these rules may seem like a lot, but they all serve an important purpose. It is crucial that the jury base its verdict only on the evidence presented during the case. To do that, jurors cannot form an opinion based on outside information.

Standard of Guilt

Before the trial begins, the judge will walk the jury through what must be proven in order for a defendant to be found guilty of any specific charges, known as the standard of guilt. This is an important part of the process because it sets out specifically what each juror must be sure of before they decide on a verdict. Some defendants have multiple charges, in which case the jury will deliberate and deliver a verdict on each one individually. This can include evidence that the defendant planned a crime ahead of time or proof of intent to cause harm in some way. It is the responsibility of the prosecution to prove this to the jurors.

Beyond a Reasonable Doubt

The phrase "beyond a reasonable doubt" is the bedrock on which the juror's decision rests. Anyone accused of a crime is believed to be innocent until proven guilty, which is why it is so important for jurors to have no prior opinion about a particular case or defendant.

In a criminal case, the burden of proof is on the prosecuting attorney, meaning she must prove a defendant's guilt beyond a reasonable doubt.

During the trial, it is the responsibility of the prosecution to prove that the defendant has committed a crime. While the defense attorney argues against that case, the burden of proof rests on the plaintiff or the state.

So what does "beyond a reasonable doubt" mean? It means that jurors can see no reasonable reason to doubt the guilt or innocence of the defendant. This is intended to make the burden of proof difficult to reach; if a juror is left with reasonable doubt, then they

Jurors in Pop Culture

Jurors and juries feature prominently in numerous TV shows, movies, and other pieces of pop culture. On shows like *Law & Order*, the jury is often anonymous; they are on camera, but they don't play an active role in the drama of the show until delivering their verdict. But in some cases, the jury and its deliberations are the primary focus of the plot. This is true of the legendary *12 Angry Men*, which originally aired on TV in 1954 before being made into a play in 1955 and a film in 1957. The story follows twelve men as they deliberate on a homicide case, for which they have been asked to use reasonable doubt as the standard of guilt. Although early on in the deliberations only one man does not think the defendant is guilty, over the course of the story more and more jurors begin to question the guilt of the defendant. The film adaptation is considered one of the best films ever made, and the stage adaptation continues to be produced today.

cannot reach a guilty verdict. But that works both ways: If there are no scenarios or doubts, then a defendant has to be found guilty.

All cases in criminal court must be proven beyond a reasonable doubt, but in civil cases the standard can be a preponderance of evidence. In these cases, the jury must find that there is enough evidence to find a defendant guilty. This standard is not considered as high as guilt beyond a reasonable doubt because all that must be proven is that the prosecution's argument is more likely than not true. Clear and convincing evidence is another standard that is more difficult to prove than a preponderance of evidence but still less difficult than guilt beyond a reasonable doubt.

All of this shapes the way the jury deliberates and what jurors have to agree upon before they can reach a verdict. It's why reaching a unanimous decision can sometimes be difficult or might never happen at all. But it's important that jurors are impartial and fair because their decisions can lead to severe punishments. It's crucial that all jurors understand what they are expected to do in order to make sure they help deliver justice.

Ensuring a Fair Trial

In the United States, juries were established in order to ensure a fair trial free from state manipulation or influence. Juries are meant to serve as a middleman between the judiciary and the citizenry, providing valuable and impartial input on cases. But access to juries has made that impartiality questionable throughout the history of the United States and has impacted the justice system for centuries. Racial, gender, and class discrimination have been present in jury selection since the earliest days of our country, and the influence of that exclusion can still be felt today.

A History of Discrimination

When the United States was founded, the full rights of citizens, including the ability to serve on juries, were given to only a select group of people. White men who owned land were the only ones allowed to serve as jurors, while women and anyone who did not own property were barred from doing so. This was also true of voting rights, which were restricted to land-owning white men as well.

This created a class bias among jurors; those who were sitting on juries were privileged and wealthy, which could change the way they saw defendants based on their class, and possible bias could influence their verdict. States were given the right to set restrictions on who could and could not serve on juries, and through the later eighteenth century and early nineteenth century, laws restricting the rights of non-property-owning white men were eliminated.

This opened up juries to citizens of all classes, but many people were still excluded based on gender and race. Men of color and women were barred from serving on juries until the nineteenth century and the twentieth century respectively, and inequality remains a huge issue in jury selection, particularly for people of color.

After the Civil War, the Fourteenth Amendment and the Civil Rights Act of 1875 gave former male slaves access to jury duty, but states began passing laws that restricted that access. In 1879, the Supreme Court ruled in *Strauder v. West Virginia* that these state laws were a violation of the Fourteenth Amendment, but subsequent decisions upheld discriminatory practices that made juries heavily white on the grounds that the racial makeup of a jury doesn't guarantee a biased verdict. After the repeal of the Civil Rights Act of 1875 and the 1896 *Plessy v. Ferguson* Supreme Court decision, which established the "separate but equal" precedent that allowed for legal discrimination, people of color were once again barred from serving on juries. Although today such discrimination is not legal at the state or federal level, racial bias is still an issue in jury selection.

Women were also barred from serving on juries for most of the country's history. This can be traced back to English law, in which women were not allowed to serve on juries because of a "defect of sex," or simply being women. In its 1880 decision in *Strauder v. West Virginia*, the Supreme Court upheld the right of states to exclude women from jury duty. Western states became the first to allow women on juries, but it wasn't until the 1920s that many other states started following suit. The Civil Rights Act of 1957 ended the exclusion of women from federal juries, but it wasn't until 1968 that women were allowed to serve on juries in all fifty states.

A Jury of One's Peers

Although not enshrined in the Constitution, the idea of a jury of one's peers has become a cornerstone of how we think about impartial juries. This is because subtle or extreme biases can influence verdicts in ways that change the lives of defendants. This can apply to any marginalized group and can have extremely negative effects on the lives of those on trial.

An example of this is the case of the Scottsboro boys, nine African American teenagers in Alabama who were accused and

Juries are meant to serve as a mediator between citizens and the judiciary.

A jury of one's peers is essential for a fair trial, reducing the possibility that someone will be convicted of a crime because of racial bias or other forms of prejudice.

convicted of raping two white women in 1931. The case was decided by an all-white jury, something that is still not illegal in the United States, that found the young boys guilty. As a result, eight of the boys were sentenced to death. But before their sentence could be carried out, the case fell apart; one of the women recanted her prior testimony during an appeal hearing, saying that they made the story up. Despite this, the jury again found the boys guilty, but the judge granted a new trial right away. After another guilty verdict, a Supreme Court case, and a full retrial, four of the nine defendants were cleared of charges. By 2013, Alabama had issued pardons—some of them posthumous—for all nine of the boys.

This is just one case in which a jury's bias influenced its decision. While it is extreme, it highlights why a jury that does not include at least a fraction of the defendant's peers, whether that be women or people of color, can work against justice rather than for it.

A Legacy of Bias

The jury system has struggled to overcome bias that was once built into the law, and equal representation for people of color and women is still not common. Jury selection allows attorneys to dismiss potential jurors for any reason—or for no reason at all. This means that jury selection can itself be discriminatory. Studies have found that people of color are often excluded from serving on juries; one 2010 study by the Equal Justice Initiative found that as of 2010, around 80 percent of qualified African American jurors[1] were dismissed from service in counties across the Deep South.

Racial bias has been a major problem in the justice system, one that can only be solved by increased diversity in all aspects of the judicial process.

Racial Bias in the Justice System

Jurors are a unique part of the justice system, often with no other links to the process in their everyday lives. But while their role is unique, as jurors they fit into a much larger whole, and it's important to understand the issues in the justice system in order to fully understand how bias on juries can impact trials. Racial bias in the justice system has been studied and debated for decades, with many studies finding that bias at all levels impacts who is accused of crimes, who is convicted, what their sentences look like, and how likely they are to return to prison after serving a jail term. Police brutality against people of color has become a national issue in recent years with high-profile killings. People of color make up a vast majority of inmates in the United States, and studies have found that African Americans receive harsher sentences than people of other races. It's not just juries that may be biased; systematic racism has created an environment in which people of color are often treated unequally. Tackling these issues and finding the root causes of racial bias are an important part of ensuring justice for all.

What Does a Juror Do?

For women, the first all-woman jury was sworn in in Los Angeles in 1911, but it is still newsworthy when it happens, as it was during George Zimmerman's trial in Florida in 2013. Zimmerman was tried for shooting an unarmed black teenager, Trayvon Martin. While the trial would have made headlines on its own, that the makeup of the jury made headlines around the country is a reminder of how far juries have come and how far we have to go before equality is not newsworthy.

The Future of Juries

Serving on a jury is a hard-fought right and a special duty. It's a chance for men and women to do their part in ensuring justice is delivered. But that doesn't mean the system is perfect. As we've learned, juries have evolved over time, and that evolution continues today. Although we've come a long way, there is still important work to be done to ensure that jurors are able to fully participate and that all juries hand down verdicts free from bias or influence outside the courtroom.

Challenging Biases

As we learned in the last chapter, biases and discrimination are a lingering issue in the jury system. Racial bias is present at all stages of the jury process, from selection to deliberation. People of color are less likely to be selected for jury service, which impacts the makeup of juries that hear cases where the defendants or plaintiffs are people of color. An example is the case of *Foster v. Chapman*, during which an all-white jury found Timothy Foster, an African

Serving on a jury is a civic duty, giving the average citizen the opportunity to participate in the justice system.

American man, guilty of murder, and he was sentenced to death. But in 2016, the Supreme Court ruled that prosecutors had purposefully excluded people of color from the jury, marking their names with a "B" and deciding which ones they would choose if they had to have "one of the black jurors" on the panel.[1] It's a cycle of exclusion that can have extreme consequences for all involved and that has been taken to the Supreme Court multiple times since the late 1800s.

But there are organizations working to overcome it, although how to do so is far from clear. The American Civil Liberties Union takes on cases involving juries at a state and national level, including cases of discrimination in jury selection or where a biased jury could have influenced a verdict. The Equal Justice Initiative also works to remove discriminatory practices in the jury system and publishes reports on its findings regarding these issues. Even the American Bar Association is involved in reversing generations of discrimination and exclusion to ensure that bias is removed from the jury system. It will take time and significant reform to ensure bias doesn't influence the jury system, but dedicated people are working toward that very future.

Making Jury Duty Possible for Everyone

For some people, serving on a jury is simply not possible due to financial or time constraints. Most courts pay only a small stipend or travel costs for one or multiple days of jury duty, and for those living on a low income taking that time off work is not affordable. Others are unable to serve because of prior obligations, a lack of child care, or other reasons. All of these issues can make jury duty an undue burden on those who are unable to get excused from service.

Groups like the American Tort Reform Association are working to change that by advocating for reforms ranging from a longer window of time when a juror won't be called for duty again to employee rights. ATRA advocates for making it easier to get exceptions or postpone service, protecting workers from losing salary or having to use leave to serve on juries, and a special fund from which long-term jurors can receive compensation. These reforms are all designed to make it easier for people to serve on juries without

Longer trials, like the eleven-month O. J. Simpson case, require jurors to spend a long period of time away from work, which can place a financial burden on those chosen to serve.

seeking exceptions and to ensure that the jury system doesn't exclude anyone by default.

Serving on a jury is an important duty that all US citizens share. From the very founding of our country, juries have been a key part of our justice system, designed to ensure protection of the individual. That doesn't mean that juries have been free of controversy or have always lived up to the lofty vision for how they function. For most of US history, juries have excluded people based on race, gender, and

Eliza Stewart Boyd: The First Woman on a Jury

In 1869, Wyoming passed legislation giving women full political rights in the state, including the right to serve on a jury. Only six months later, in March 1870, Eliza Stewart Boyd became the first woman selected for jury duty in the United States, serving as a juror on a grand jury just a few weeks before another group of women were the first selected to serve on a trial jury. Although Boyd's selection was at random, her role as the first woman to serve on a jury was fitting. She was the first teacher to work in the public school system in Laramie, Wyoming, and spent most of her adult life advocating for women's rights and the expansion of the arts. Three years after serving as a juror, Boyd became the first woman nominee for territorial legislature in Wyoming, although she did not accept. Today, she is remembered as a trailblazer, thanks in large part to her service to her community as a juror and activist.

All United States citizens are called to appear for jury duty, even famous and important figures like former president Barack Obama.

class, and that troubled history has left behind a legacy of bias and discrimination.

Juries, like every other part of our nation, have been in a constant state of evolution, and that is still true today. Proposed reforms are aimed at making sure that everyone, regardless of race, gender, or employment, is able to take part in the justice process. Jurors help safeguard the rule of law, and doing so is a right and responsibility all citizens should have a chance to experience.

CHAPTER NOTES

Chapter 1. The History of the Jury

1. "Amendment VI: Speedy Public Trial by Jury," the Rutherford Institute, https://www.rutherford.org/constitutional_corner/amendment_vi_speedy_public_trial_by_jury.

Chapter 2. A Day as a Juror

1. Michael Tackett, "Nation's Longest Civil Jury Trial Winds Down," *Chicago Tribune*, September 6, 1987, http://articles.chicagotribune.com/1987-09-06/news/8703070473_1_david-snively-dioxin-monsanto.

Chapter 4. Ensuring a Fair Trial

1. "Study: Blacks Routinely Excluded from Juries," NPR, June 20, 2010, http://www.npr.org/templates/story/story.php?storyId=127969511.

Chapter 5. The Future of Juries

1. Steven Bright, "How Supreme Court Fixed a Racial Wrong," CNN .com, May 23, 2016, http://www.cnn.com/2016/05/23/opinions/supreme-court-black-jurors-bright/index.html.

GLOSSARY

burden of proof The obligation to prove an argument with evidence.

citizen An individual legally recognized as a national of a state.

defense The legal team working for a defendant or accused party.

deliberation The process by which a jury discusses a case and reaches a verdict in private.

empaneled Sworn in for a case.

evidence Testimony, objects, or other items presented to a court in support of a case.

grand jury A panel that listens to evidence to determine the validity of charges before a trial.

hung jury A jury that cannot agree on a verdict.

juror A person sworn in to serve on a jury during a trial.

jury A panel, usually of twelve people, that hears the evidence of a case and reaches a verdict.

justice system The agencies and courts that enact the law.

mistrial A trial in which an error has taken place, making it necessary to start a new trial.

prosecution The legal team working to prove a case on behalf of a plaintiff or the state.

trial by ordeal An ancient system wherein someone accused of a crime would be tested through physical tasks.

unanimous A unanimous decision is one on which everyone agrees.

verdict The final decision a jury reaches regarding guilt in a case.

Books

Hale, Dennis. *The Jury in America: Triumph and Decline.* Lawrence, KS: University Press of Kansas, 2016.

Kowalski, Kathiann M., *Judges and Courts: A Look at the Judicial Branch.* Minneapolis, MN: Lerner Publications, 2012.

Murray, Hallie. *The Right to a Jury Trial: The Seventh Amendment.* New York, NY: Enslow Publishing, 2017.

Websites

American Civil Liberties Union

www.aclu.org

National nonprofit organization with reports and information about the justice system and juries.

United States Courts

www.uscourts.gov

Federal website with information about jury service, types of jury trials, and other topics.

INDEX